Dolores:
The Alpine Years

PANSY MAURER-ALVAREZ

Hanging Loose Press
Brooklyn, New York

Published by Hanging Loose Press, 231 Wyckoff Street, Brooklyn, NY 11217. All rights reserved. No part of this book may be reproduced without the publisher's written permission, except for brief quotations in reviews.

Printed in the United States of America
10 9 8 7 6 5 4 3 2 1

Some of these poems first appeared in the following publications: *Hanging Loose* (U.S.A.); *Pharos; Staple* (U.K.); *The Observer/Arvon Poetry Collection 1993* (Guardian Newspapers Ltd., U.K.)

Hanging Loose Press thanks the Fund for Poetry and the Literature Programs of the National Endowment for the Arts and the New York State Council on the Arts for grants in support of the publication of this book.

Special thanks from the author to Prof. Dr. Max Nänny and Alice Notley for encouragement, criticism and kindness. And to Christian for that and even more.

Cover art by Robin Tewes
Cover design by Caroline Drabik

Library of Congress Cataloging-in-Publication Data

Maurer-Alvarez, Pansy
        Dolores : the alpine years / Pansy Maurer-Alvarez.
        p.   cm.
        ISBN 1-882413-31-8 (cloth). -- ISBN 1-882413-30-X (pbk.)
        I. Title.
PS 3563.A884D65   1996
811'.54--dc20   95-49708
                                            CIP

Produced at The Print Center, Inc., 225 Varick St., New York, NY 10014, a non-profit facility for literary and arts-related publications. (212) 206-8465

CONTENTS

for Christine Merki-Perriard
in memory

This book is a series of poems narrated by a fictitious character, a dental hygienist from Pennsylvania who lives, works and tries to love (and then does) in Switzerland.

"I do not believe in the legends of food,
I believe in the food.
It is not what carrots are like,
It is the carrots."

James Schuyler

"to have been so happy is a promise
and if it isn't kept that doesn't matter."

James Schuyler

Song

Maps of deserts, maps of mountains;
        I love maps for their colors,
                their legends, lines and borders,
    especially road maps to show you
        choices — how to get there, what
                  to avoid.
        Lines. Lines on the paper; you can rely
on their widths, the widths of roads;
        (You take the high road and I'll etc.).
Broad flat
    fast lines or, here and there squirming
                wanderlust lines that end
    in dead ends at the tops of mountains with
        restlessly no place to go; so
up a mountain, down a mountain, hill and vale.
    Swing onto wide
bypasses, orbitals and roundabouts too fast;
        check interstate numbers, ferry times,
    flight routes sometimes. Desert song, somebody's
                car radio
        with mountaineering songs.
Now back to the backs of maps for
        speed limits, exits
            and signs to get you there.
Where there? Why there?
        How, before you go; or how long, with a suitcase?
The lines are patient, keep telling you
        it's all in the maps, it's all there.

Starting from Eastern Pennsylvania

neighbors (one after the other)
buy a vacation trailer
drive west with the kids
takes a *whole* week just to get there
has become fashionable

"we've
been to California"
"so've we
haven't you ever
been to California?"
no
I say
no and no and no
to California
(one summer my parents
get us in the car
drive an hour or so
east)

"Florida? ever
been to Florida?"
no
I say
I've been to Washington
(D.C.)
"doesn't count"

                    *

one day
I wake up
go east
and east and east
on a plane

                    *

the Lake of Zurich lies
at an angle, it seems
from up here on Züriberg.
A single boat,
precise
as a surgeon's scalpel, cuts
the blue vinyl sheet
stretching across the valley,
and makes no sound

Hot Weather Blues for Limmatquai

Sunshine
muggy and windows wide—
another day
so hot you'll feel your heartbeat, heavily
till sundown;
people will surely be wanting rain.
The brain
works, but in a different mode;
on a day like this
you could easily lose your footing.

Down Limmatquai
on my way to a half day of work
(and the trams
don't seem to be getting anywhere either),
a swarm
of small shops rises and falls with the heat.
The 60's/70's
are back in fashion, but I'm not sure
we're not
over-rating an era, like we still do
fin-de-siècle or
the Impressionists with their museums, which
I like
but it can get out of hand while
waiting
in line in long-weekend Paris.

I guess living
an era on a day-to-day basis means
you miss
so much of what comes out later.
As for people
like the Impressionists, they leave you
with the seeming
impossibility of ever writing anything
new in good weather
in a park, the woods, by the sea, on a river bank
or anywhere near

a black, wrought iron balcony; so damn them
                          all
Manet, Monet, et, et, et cetera for getting
                          that trick
about globs of paint posing as light just right.

                    Travel posters of
Palladian fronts and costumes native
                    of anywhere but here—
and the very thought of my late breakfast
                    Müesli
seems poetic; maybe I should write about
                    all those little
grains of goodness soaking up all that
                    lyrical milk
while slices of bright, fresh fruit
                    provide
pleasure for the eye and vital substances
                    for the body.
To hell with it — I'll write my poem
                    written in a
Parisian park kind of poem with its own
                    new twist yet,
just give me lots of paper and a bit of time;
                    but on a day
like this you'll have to settle for
                    a 4 o'clock
coffee-break blues. Trouble with doing
                    afternoons is
you get those fast-breathing people who went
                    home for lunch
to an onion sandwich with lots of pepper
                    and beer.

The other day a man told me you could edit
                    large passages
of Mozart and not lose a thing. (What
                    not a note?)
How dare these people? Could they even
                    be right?
Maybe the heat's melting my
                    perception, maybe
this is simply a summer bad mood.

                    Good to
get down to something practical
                    like scraping the
hardened, harvest-moon cheesy-colored
                    buildup
off the stained teeth of solid city merchants
                    who like to
pretend/swear/carry on to me about
                    how they brush
regularly, in the fashion that they learned
                    from me.

This Sure Isn't the Pennsylvania Turnpike

You're doing the driving and it's real smooth the way we're
    zipping along
at 150 km/hr, way past a clear midnight.
But nothing's actually clear

    BECAUSE

it hasn't happened yet and how would I know
it's coming? The only thing that keeps coming
is the passing line of white staccatos. More regular than breathing
and much faster.
The only reason that I'm not talking is

    BECAUSE

I'm too tired to.
I put my feet up on the dashboard

    BECAUSE

they're swollen and burn from walking all over the place in the heat.
The passing line's perfectly insistent,
like it can't believe the way we keep eating it up
in front and shitting it out the back. It keeps coming
like it doesn't know what's happening. And yet, by now it must

    BECAUSE

we've been doing this for over an hour already.
I've got this indecisive feeling poking
around in my intestines looking for a place to snuggle up in,
you know like to prepare for the great combust.
You were hungry and wanted a man-pleasing meal. And
we drank a lot,
beer

    BECAUSE

you were thirsty

    BECAUSE

of the heat.
I'm getting horny with my feet
up on the dashboard like this. My legs
look kind of nice in the dark. But it's like you're not even here

BECAUSE

you're not saying anything and I can't hear
your breathing

BECAUSE

of the way the car's rumbling.
We can't stop until the highway stops. I bet
you wouldn't even stop if I had to go to the bathroom.
At customs we stopped; you turned up the radio,
so we listened to "Midnight Reveries"

BECAUSE

that's about the time it was.
We had to wait a while in line

BECAUSE

there were all these vacationers with trailers,
traveling at night to avoid the heat and the traffic. And there we were,
no luggage,
just the clothes on our backs and a tank of gas

BECAUSE

you came in yesterday afternoon late and said,
"Hey, get in the car. Let's cross some borders." So hey, wow, off we
   went
just driving, driving and driving and then we were in France.
That's where we came across that church. Eleventh century.
You weren't about to go in and have a look

BECAUSE

Hell, I'm not religious either, but just a look?
You were in a bad mood

ON ACCOUNT OF

my going in anyway.
It was special in there. Heavy with cool, like the air outside was
    heavy with heat.
You could walk around, round and around

BECAUSE

it was octagonal. So I did.
There were galleries way up high
that went round, round and around. With pale turquoise frescoes.
It reminded me of some place we'd been, some place in Salzburg.
I ran my hands over the columns

BECAUSE

no one was in there praying or anything.
I held the inside of my thigh against a column

BECAUSE

I was alone.
It felt good, cool and massive.
"Man! This place wouldn't fall down in a hurry," is what I was
    thinking.
Then I thought I'd better get back outside

BECAUSE

you'd be waiting. But you weren't there.
I walked around the parking lot and all around the church, poking
in the bushes

BECAUSE

you might think it'd be fun to hide
and jump out at me. Apparently, you weren't thinking
along those lines. So I walked into the village. Walked
all up and down the side streets, too. And the whole
way back to the church. You said you went for a beer

BECAUSE

it was so hot and you got talking to this guy. Long talk!
But I didn't say that so as not to spoil the day.
Then you wanted to go for a walk. A what?
Through pre-harvest fields

BECAUSE

of the sunset and

BECAUSE

we live in the gray heart of a city. Okay, so
this is supposed to be romantic, like bucolic. Like bull!
A haystack, exciting? Just plain prickly,
if you ask me, except that you didn't.
You felt real good afterwards and wanted a man-pleasing meal.
Alsatian Sauerkraut. In summer?
Menu touristique: big helping, cheap. So, okay.
We drank a lot

BECAUSE

you were still thirsty.
Around midnight we crossed back into Switzerland
with nothing to declare.
That was before you said it.
That there was no point. No point in going on.
We're going on all right, on, on and on

BECAUSE

that's where the road's going and we haven't eaten up all the
    staccatos yet.
No point.

BECAUSE

you can't stand it anymore.
I don't get that. It's what I've been doing all along, but I don't say this

BECAUSE

I see there's no point. It has happened.

Pick A Color

Blue.

Blue was the color of the bottom
of the boat, the glass
boat-shaped object
called *Objet* that had
tiny, two-dimensional
women floating
in the solidified glass
that filled its hull as
it sat
in a spotlight
alone.

Blue
was the color of Kath's
scarf with black and brown
when she took me to
the glass gallery to see *Objet*
with its tiny two-
dimensional female
figures drowning in the
water which was glass
filling the bottom of the narrow boat
in the spotlight
alone.

Blue was
the color of Kath's rage
in the glass gallery
when she saw and
as she said, "We can't
even nail the bastard for
misrepresentation." —
the artist was present
and surrounded
by women. And
all his other
objects, called *Madre*,

Vessel, called *Objet III*
or *IX*, etc. were
in spotlights, silent,
were women, alone and
blue of color.

Spiral Notebooks

I wrote a list and circled
key elements:
noodles and chocolate
flowers (blue)
nail polish (orange)
olive oil.
Friends are important, I wrote:
invite Veronique
call Urs
try Fred, too
see Kath, if possible
this week—
call Sibyl again.
I need to feel the seasons
so started another list:
Ticino
magnolias, earlier
camellias
tiramisù ice cream cones
lakes
palm trees and
quatro stagione
Where would we be without wine?
Twilight?
Wind off the lake?
Or sentimentality?
And I immediately saw I was
making a mental list:
try to get up earlier
work harder, talk
less, eat healthier
walk more
maybe jog
(Oh God!)
I'd need to get running shoes
and something to wear
a headband and
that would be yet
another list.

I like lots of
quiet things in
between:
browsing for art-reproduction
post cards, blank books
purple
ink and shoes.
The moon turns me on and I need
the sun and the stars
equally.
I like all of Beethoven
Italo-Hits (any decade)
the Schubert Impromptus
and most of Mozart, the fragrance
of the three blue hyacinths
on my table. (I've just
made Mozart hyacinth
blue, poor thing!
Rossini's red and
Verdi's green.) Oh no,
that's silly!
Maybe I like being silly.
Try to be silly more often.
I am never happy with:
my hair
my usual weekend arrangements
my fondue (cheese)
my inability to work my creative
energy into neat regular parcels
I'm stopping this list from getting longer.
How about colors:
cobalt
vermilion, except
it sounds like a combination of
"vermin" and "venereal"
all purples, violets, lilacs
some greens— emerald, esp. with
black,
shocking greens, spring greens
occasionally mints, turquoisy
greens
no olives.
Places to go if/when money comes in:

down the Nile
in the moonlight
with a man or a friend
well, down the Nile, anyway
Lanzarote, just to lie in black sand
Pompeii
for delicate blues in the frescoes
the high road between
Monte Carlo and Nice
(the one in the movies) if
it really exists, for the view
a train south
the tamer places from
the National Geographic
I'll leave a little space and
look for some:

—

——

———

Pennsylvania rivers I can list without
having to think twice:
Monongahela
Allegheny
Brandywine
Schuylkill
Susquehanna
the Conestoga and the Delaware.
Passes, without thinking twice:
Simplon, Grimsel, Furka
Oberalp
Great St. Bernhard
San Bernadino
Bernina and Brünig
of course, St. Gotthard.
Names like:
Lamborghini, Respighi
Lago Maggiore.
Sculptural areas of the body I can't resist:
neck/collar bone/shoulder
armpit to hip (from the back)
upper, inner knee
hands, inside and out
what some sculptors do with

fingers, but rarely toes
foreheads
ears and lips
lips, also in paintings
but not only in paintings.
I feel dinner coming on:
candles
Beethoven
pinot gris
salad and shrimp.

A Simple Statement About Hochnebel

definition:

From November through February, Hochnebel, that
solid puffy lid, hovers above the city; it keeps out
the sun, keeps off the snow; wiggles its bottom at us,
settles in, spreading that huge pearl-grey ass evenly
over the Mittelland and laughs. There are other days,
exceptional, actually clear, but for the most part, this
laughing keeps up from November through February.

effect:

Somedays I feel like I'm someone's beret.
A beret has no will of its own, can be:

pulled down over the right ear
            or
down over the left
            or
tweaked into shape all fluted with dents
            or
pushed far back off the forehead
            or
pulled unbecomingly down all round
            or
worn like the cap of a mushroom.

A beret
is:

made of wool (or should be)
            and
warm
            and
comes in:

any color imaginable
(How about mint? Why not purple?)
            and
any size imaginable;

can be:
worn matching
                or
contrasting,

but is:

traditionally black, anyway dark
(if worn by men)
                and
more easily removed than put on
right.

situation:

The sky is pearl-grey and Hochnebel's laughing real hard
and solid. Up by Einsiedeln, I know the sun is strong, making
all the difference in the world; and if the Sihlsee freezes over,
there will be children and dogs playing on it -- people sunning
themselves and watching. But I feel like a beret, traditionally
dark, that someone else has pulled way down all round.

Like Grand Central Station

Kath's changed her name
    to Fedora, which makes
people think of hats and that's not far off,
    since what she does is hair.

Sibyl's busy, so busy, too busy.

Dorli is starting
    her final diet
with a doctor.

Veronique retouches,
    retouches, touches and
then has to retouch, with extra
    care, her crimson lips.

Marta doesn't want glasses-- no way, not yet, no thank *you.*
    Emma's taking driving lessons
as therapy and Monika's taking
    voice from a baritone, evenings and Sibyl...?
Sibyl's Sibyl.

Gabi's having a baby
    she thinks. Fedora
phones me for a drink and I get
    confused until I get it right.

Vreni wants a man *so bad* she's
    trying typing
after work, which we all tell her
    will never work.

I notice it's full moon and
    rather beautiful out tonight.

Petra's exhibiting in a gallery
    near the lake and I
was thinking of throwing a midnight
    finissage-sort-of-party for her

but Dorli has to massage her boy's muscles
        after practice and Marta
says she doesn't, well, really know; Gabi's
        out and Veronique is out of town, I know.
Vreni can't admit she can't
        come along alone
and Emma's therapy isn't working
        at all. Sibyl's
line's still busy. I call up Fedora,
        call her Kath and she
corrects me and says we'll have the best
        midnight finissage surprise yet, just the three of us,
"Don't you worry yourself, Starlight!"
        she says.

Angles in the Alpine Mode

It's midsummer —
         up here
at the edge of a mountainside I'm
in the middle of spring flowers
         pink, white and
Alpine. The small
         of my back is cold from the
walking through the woods kind of sweat
collected since this p.m.
still sticking.
The sun's going down, the alp's getting damp,
get up before it's not good for your back
         (I have a bad back) and now slowly
an altitude pressure headache.
I'm in what could
         look like
the edge of the world kind of photograph,
the about ready to get up and jump/roll/slide/step
off
all depending on the
angle from where you are type of photo
         (not art photography), so this guy
snaps that kind of photo
of me.
Ever read those stories
         (hear those jokes) about people
who take pictures of people in
         positions like mine
at this moment, on this alp, they say "Look into
the lens", they say " a little
to the right, one step
         back and gotcha!"
I need some more aspirin and want
to get back alone.

Bobby Bongo

turns his radio
to the samba station and serves
mineral water, Coke (regular or light), Gini
or anything else that comes in bottles or cans.

Truck tires painted pink
mark off Café Bongo-Bongo
from the beach and the marsh ditches—
pink (Pepto-Bismol pink) to match the shack.

Every sunny day since
I've come to this unused part
of Mediterranean coast, I sit in the shade
of this man's shack, drink something, just to watch

the wind froth out
his long, long pony tail,
sweep the crown of his head like wind
across a field of sparsely planted, ripening wheat.

The samba station,
the slap of his flip-flops,
the rattle of his turquoise plastic bead curtain and
the privilege of staring straight through my sunglasses

at his profile
turned towards the sea,
make up for the fact that
he has never said a word to me, except

to indicate
the price of what I consume.
Suits me fine. But when the wind
comes down from the persistent north,

it does not come kindly.
Then, it's a cruel walk out
across marshland paths towards the
plywood gorilla and palm tree atop the shack;

they get the shakes
and the gale gives me earache.
My feet crunch salt-crusted sand
in rhythm— malata ... d'amore, malata ... d'amore.

Bobby Bongo rolls
another cigarette and
faces the Mediterranean—
a proud, weathered man, standing upright

at the prow
of his pink shack,
holding his own against the wind,
watching young men in tight suits test

their cunning,
their grace and reflexes
against the wind and what
it does to the water when they're in it.

Bobby Bongo picks up
his radio (and we both know this
comes from his heart), moves it down the counter
towards me, lets the sambas play and play for me alone.

Rear View

Difficult exercise:
what should a poem about a best friend be about ?
    Overlapping degrees of good-better-best;
shifting sands, maybe rock; winds from Zephyr to Föhn,
    Mistral,
Sirocco and the whole way back again; or swerves,
about-faces, near-misses, head-on collisions. Well, this

    is about Fedora's rear view.
She's got a problem with it, stuck on her windshield
right up in front of her eyes; gets so riveted
to some spot that's slipped away from her,
    it's just a speck
behind us in the streetscape; her eyes
are bloodshot with the strain of it all. I tell her
    she's missing all the large, exciting
stuff, like trams, coming at us fast up front.
    She can't hear

and she won't stop hollering about her timetable and people
who're trying to line something up for her. I don't like

this acceleration, her mental hopscotch, these
haphazard intersections; I could use some peace:
    home, earphones, Victor Kaiser — and
listen as he takes a solid hold of
    "Monk's Lobsterpot",
leans into that piano, refines the theme; I'd put him
on the permanent repeat button. But what's required

of me, I'd like to know, here during the process of a
noisy red light on
    Seilergraben towards Central?
On green, I finally get through and say, "The real
problem, Fedora, is you're so afraid Beat'll
find someone new before *you* do." And wham,
slam—the brakes, the cursing and the whole bit.

4 Hospital Poems

fluorescent moon   no, a light
hospital, I'm told
is, I think   immense building with people
pushing beds and
buckets along corridors   day and night
I begin   to name things   find something
I recognize and name it
ceremoniously, pain
nurses and other people   look in on me   lots
have name tags   Schwester Angelika   Schwester Sabine
male nurses are not
called brothers   they wash me
gently   all over with warm water and
take more time to answer   questions while
my mind steers away from people
in other arteries and   cells of the building
what they're here for   what the others do
lots of washing going on in the basement
in washing machines
sheets and gowns, boiling   going round and around
in dryers   everything
feels so light   the floor bounces

***

My dreams are thick and heavy
like applesauce: I'm on the operating table
vaguely awake and they're removing tiny
creatures by the dozens from me;
in place of legs these have
curled-up tails like baby ferns.
One nurse says, "They're beautiful baby mermaids!"
Explains the tails will strengthen with time
and grow magnificent
glimmering fins that I'll be proud of. The doctor isn't
pleased, says they're frightened and hardly breathing and if
I can't do any better, he'll have to
give me something. I'm dreaming
as I wake, that my room is full

of colorful Easter baskets, each with a tiny
creature in it, dead.

***

Heat in a haze quivers over the lake;
    I'm pasted to the sheets with sweat again.
Siegfried and Schwester Ursi
    bend in unison, without hurting me much,
change the bed -- his sex nestles
    behind uniform white buttons
on level with my good hand, hardly
    out of reach. Last night my line-up
of Get Well cards gained ground on me
    when I wasn't looking; I drifted
in and out of a summer
    thunderstorm, watched yellow
storm-warning lights flash across the lake.
    I've formed a habit of listening
to "Casta Diva" and John Surman while
    watching the lake at night.

***

Finally my last day and dessert
is a pink fruit mousse
again, sweating profusely.

Frau Hugentobler, from the next room, says
she was sick, it was the Birchermüesli
didn't agree with her at all
kept repeating on her, then smack in the middle
of the night, it went SPLAT, just like that, all
over the floor, got in the cracks, stank, she couldn't help it;
you could still make out the strawberry halves
(maybe it *was* the strawberries)
and one of those nice night boys had to come and clean it up.
Her husband, Ernst
drove her into a cow pasture up
in Unterägeri, put her whole right side out of whack
and all *he* got was scratches, the old fart.

Detail of a Girl

A detail of Sir John Lavery's *Girl
in a Red Dress Reading by a Swimming Pool*
covers a paperback

on Fedora's table and gets
me thinking about those three-dimensional
torsos on male swimmers in

contests, such as the Olympics, that I
sometimes catch parts of
on my diminutive (What a pity!), two-

dimensional screen.
I think a while about muscles in
general (male, female)

then muscles and music in particular
and how you can't hear them
when they play.

I remember Pennsylvania and music,
Mount Gretna, mosquito evenings
and how my mother

made gathered skirts in
clean red and white florals,
weighted down by several rows

of rickrack at the hem.
I wore them, even
to school. (I had begun to master the

piano here and there, sometimes
in public, on peoples' uprights,
on request, and I was way beyond

rickrack.) Once
someone, beaming, in Pennsylvania,
told me, after my rendition of

"Gertrude's Dream Waltz"
or maybe Schubert's"Serenade",
at the Asa Packer

Mansion up in Jim Thorpe,
that I had played
the grand like a man.

I was rooted to the parquet, in something
gathered and red, with a mighty
statement of rickrack round the hem.

Darlene's

When I was a few years out of kneesocks and saddle shoes,
    A-cups and Clearasil, I found myself
Well into bell-bottoms and a date out on a Saturday, out in a
    pickup, looking out for spare parts.

We stopped at DARLENE'S up near the interstate round about
    lunch. Now, DARLENE'S
Was a one-woman concern, except when her aging mom came in to
    help peel eggs.

Everyone around knew DARLENE'S; it's where you'd go after the
    movies with your girl-
Friends or boyfriend and narrow your choice down to DAR-
    LENE'S Death-by-Chocolate, her

Peanut Butter Cheesecake, that made your tongue stick to the roof
    of your mouth for days on end, or
DARLENE'S Own Chocolate Mint Brownies, just about as black as
    her Death and so permeated

With mint, you could have used them for mouthwash; you'd have
    to start kissing real hard after
One of DARLENE'S mint brownies just to get the feeling back in
    your lips, tongue and taste buds.

DARLENE'S served such a hefty chowder you could stand your
    spoon up in it and you got plenty
Of crackers along side. She herself was skin and bone, being a one-
    woman concern six days a week.

The oldies-but-goodies would go out for a Sundae or a Split in
    summer. Everybody ended up at
DARLENE'S at one point or other in life. But it wasn't really a
    family place because DARLENE'S

Was small and always packed so you had to not be in a hurry for
    your food. My pickup truck
Guy ordered a sub. Now DARLENE'S subs were the biggest,
    longest, highest-piled

For miles around. You had to really work hard to get your mouth
around one of DARLENE'S
Subs. It was the kind of belch-accompanying accomplishment men
in my parts were real proud of.

I ordered a salad bowl. Not the Gardener's Bowl, that had the
beets, corn, carrots, the tomatoes,
Potatoes, peppers, onions and slaw on a deep bed of fresh lettuce,
but DARLENE'S Own Special Bowl,

With the beets, carrots, corn, hard-boiled egg, the onions, peppers,
potatoes, tomatoes and,
Instead of the slaw, a mound of Dairy Maid cottage cheese. The
Dairy Maid van used to be out

In front of DARLENE'S lots, especially in summer when she could
hardly keep up. That Saturday,
I looked down at my deep, luscious bowl, crowned with my
favorite dairy product and there,

Right in the middle of my pristine mound, like a cherry on the
fluffy pinnacle of a DARLENE'S
Sundae, was the thickest, blackest, longest, shiniest, pubic hair I
had ever come into such close

Contact with, out of context, that is. My spare-part date looked,
then looked away; he had black hair.
I didn't, don't and never will, anywhere. The woman who ran
DARLENE'S was a redhead, dyed

Somewhere between "Venetian Renaissance Copper" and "Rich
Oriental Plum," worked up into a high-rise
That shone like patent leather in a spotlight. Could this specimen
have conceivably come from anywhere

On her pale, overworked body? Anyway, I was sure it was male.
So, where did it float in from? Who
Was hiding out in DARLENE'S kitchen? The puny Dairy Maid
man? Now we've all eaten a hair,

At one point or another, our own or the dog's, in the soup or the
   stew. Bet we've had fingernails, too,
No doubt in deep-fried crab cakes (although hardly at DAR-
   LENE'S) and just thought they were

Bits of shell; could have even had their own dirt deep-fried along
   with them. Sitting at DARLENE'S
That Saturday round noon, I was imbued with my newfound,
   braless bravado; I maneuvered my prize

Hair onto my fork, raised it to my lips and closed my mouth, ever
   so licentiously, around it. It didn't
Taste of anything. My date stared, mid-bite. My mother, who
   approved of DARLENE'S high standard

Of hygiene, would have shrieked, "Spit it out! Quick! You don't
   know where it's been!" Oh, but I did.
I knew exactly where it belonged, just not on whom. There I was
   eating pubic hair in public and all I could

Think of was what my mother would have said! "Spare Parts"
   started applying himself with extra vigor
To his DARLENE'S Super Sub, trying not to watch me munch and
   crunch around on my hair. Was I

Proving too much of a woman for him? Right there in one of
   DARLENE'S booths? Just as well his mouth
Was stuffed with sub. But I was having a hard time; my hair
   wouldn't split either crosswise or lengthwise.

Male, I thought, so unbending (this, too, was newfound). The
   woman we all called DARLENE came by
To ask if everything was okay. "Great bowl," I said. In the end, of
   course, I swallowed the hair whole

Because you can't turn around on a one-lane, one-way street, not at
   DARLENE'S, not anywhere. But
You can look back and I sometimes wonder if that hair in all its
   shining tenacity wasn't female after all.

Midday Paris Saturday

Just as you wake up and start thinking this certain
                    person
            is sort of becoming
                    part
of your daily activities, you see this scene:

            men out there in the street, young,
            in the sun in the street— dark suits,
            polished shoes, precise haircuts.

Across from the hotel, large white underwear
            hangs at an attic window,
                    crisp
                    against the clear September
sky. This is not a trompe-l'oeil backdrop. You think
you'll watch, have another brioche.
                            Coffee.

            The men's fingers are deep in
white fluffy bows of dotted-Swiss
                            netting. Tulle. The men
are talking softly, smiling, taping the bows and
                    white,
            white satin roses to the windshield wipers
and radio antennas of their large
                            sparkling cars.

A middle-aged woman up
        by the laundry, looks down, smiles,
decides apparently to
        watch, too — glorious wedding
                    weather, wonderful
            morning.
She watches and smiles and
                    nods like a silly
        felt dog on a dashboard. You want to
                    run
        from folly or
                something much bigger.

So you leave the scene, at the end of
Act One, as it were, leave
the big woman watching and nodding,
before
the men can look up or
the bride comes out with her
women in hot
pulsating colors; you leave the young men
still calm in the street,
talking, arranging, taping, preparing, smiling— their teeth
as white as their shirts.

With other streets around you
later, you forget until
night and you're about to try,
again, to fall
asleep in your pale peach satin nightie with
black polka dots, which *he*
gave you and which is, without
a doubt,
too tight under the arms, you see persistently:

those men in the street intent on their bows
and roses, smiling, and the woman, whose
underwear striped the sky, smiling, nodding.

Almost As Perfect As Beethoven's 7th

Beethoven! Ah, the valor
of the man to start his 7th like that!
The verve! My favorite
of all starts; but with a man
like Beethoven
how could you have one favorite!

I, too, know my job, but in my
case, that's sometimes the trouble — there goes
another potential
relationship, swirling
down the stainless steel drain.
You see, I drive men off: they say
my eyes have fingers
busy with a curette; they fear a sharp, quick
flick of the wrist , they want to scream, gingiva
bleeding at the mere thought.
It all but drives them up the Eiger Nordwand blindfolded.

Did Beethoven take his
job to bed? If so, the sex
must have been perfection.

Once a man tried to drive me
into a rainbow's end in a rented car
up in Scotland — that would have been perfection —
by the moor, the lackadaisical sheep
but suddenly there were a lot of explanations and
no more condoms.

It isn't my thinking
of these other men, during
moments of a weekend assignation
how we drove almost to Lausanne, circling the slow
curve of Lac Léman before I realized, insignificantly,
the absence of telephone poles everywhere
that ruins the best of them; I'm just not
a D.H. with blurry bedroom vision.
Ah, the Poco sostenuto—vivace!

Yes, my favorite of all starts.
Then the Allegretto.
Back, the lover's head
and shoulders arch back, strain —
his mouth opens
in joy, triumphant release, whatever, who cares, and there
it is: all
his plaque laid
unsuspectingly, in front of me —
lined up in a neat semicircle across the stage
like the chorus in *Nabucco*,
and can I let it be? This man is
going to have monumental
periodontal trouble up ahead. If you care
about a man, why can't you care about his teeth?
Can't a woman
be good at her job?
There's suddenly lots of explaining,
(So when is
the right moment to mention it? When else
would I have seen it ?)
and I end up with one
steaming mad Swiss, leaving.

I put on the 7th
Oh, help me, Maestro!
but I'm too far gone; I'm almost chanting
"Floss, Baby, floss" and asking
So how many of your own teeth did you
have left?

I Slept Through the Rush Hour Alone

It says ten
fifty-three in red
ruby numerals by my shoulder.
Outside, cars.
I've been hoping for snow
all December but know the sound
is only more
and more rain. In the room
beneath my bed a woman
well over eighty is learning the "Barcarole",
hasn't got its rocking
gondolas right yet; searching,
scrambling over most of the
keys available, she must
make some quick decisions. This
is called sight-reading.
A plane, the eleven o'clock
church bells, cars
and now "Moonlight Sonata" (as always
first movement only) — the cup
of tea I get
out of bed to make, add saccharin but no
cream, is my conscientious
effort away from
bad lonely-bed habits — a bar
of Swiss chocolate
with almonds
is just plain
atrocious bed behaviour. Granted, it only cost
1 Franken 80 and that's cheap in anybody's
book for immediate, sweet,
creamy and soft
company.

Opera Poem

A large, dark gilt cavern — it all begins in the dark, with
    Lighting engineers, a mandolinist
Under special contract. You move, liltingly,
    Through the recitative to the next aria/duet/or
Whatever it's going to be with this list of jumbled
    Figures: a donna this, a donna that, Zerlina, a Giovanni
And one don more, a servant, etc., a farmer,
    A whole horde of farmers. Oh, the little explosions!
Mix but don't match properly or there'd be no
    Dramatic reason to have added all the music;
And don't forget the irate, Latin, ranting father, that extra dash
    Of parental pepper. Above all, make them sing! Sing!
They bring on a woman in a sedan-chair— where? Oh! Where
    Are we going from here? But it won't be for long,
Things are moving fast — thirty-second notes at least. And,
    By the way, who is the prima donna? Or rather, who thinks
She is? This could get very, very sticky indeed, especially
    Backstage. Velvets and taffetas heat up/go damp with
So much diaphragmic exertion — the itch under the
    Wig, the armpits, the spread of the itch
In the crotch of those shiny, red, Latex tights — all
    In the cruel line of spotlight fire;
Running around, or rather, back and forth, fretting about:
    Giving your hand to a man like D.G., or
Coming to the window (if you think you hear soft singing);
    Or about farmer husbands on
Wedding days — Sospiro, oh! — bridal froth, peasant beer
    And happiest day stuff.
Above all, sing; keep singing. Sing your heart out,
    Your soul out, your lungs out, your mental health,
Family and friends out, out closest relative.
    Of course, you're loving every nuance of it
In your operatic purple up here in the dark, with
    your costume party earrings, Eau de Pivoine
And fatal love affair stab the mezzo in the heart
    Red nail polish (no, sorry, wrong opera).
What got into M. when he wrote this? Giving Don O.
    Such an divine aria?

How many mild men does a woman want in her
    Life at one Moment? It's getting on your nerves,
On behalf of millions of other fine women.
    Ach! Bellyaching to yourself at the opera,
While Don G.'s doing a great job, singing the
    Gold leaf right off the rafters.
Intermission with champagne and warmed
    Schinkengipfeli
On the roof towards the newspaper offices, or else the
    lake — storm-warning lights flashing
Yellow across the lake from Wollishofen
    The night of *Rigoletto.*
Anyone you know? Nice to see women who had once
    Been wives that stayed home
Evenings with children. Oh, D.G.,
    That overcooked topic! He's changed
His clothes for another feast and they bring on lots of
    Extra boobs to run and jump and wiggle.
Across the horseshoe curve of a top balcony, the clean-cut
    Little man, who stumbled on your scarf earlier,
Has got his glasses on you, as though he belonged
    In that art reproduction postcard by
Mary Cassatt — watch out, this could be dangerous;
    remember — How many mild men
Does a woman, etc., etc.? He works somewhere clean,
    Lives tastefully, you bet conducts Strauss (Richard)
On his living-room sound system and loves his nipples,
    Ritualistically, every morning in the shower.
Don Giovanni's going to hell, slowly, still singing beautifully.
    What does his voice look like without the wig?
All those women down there, or out there for that matter,
    Moaning around about one bad man with
Perfect teeth and thighs, while
    Don Ottavio in
Elevated boots, or the clean little man with manners, stand
    In the wings, waiting patiently to be made use of.
It's all fire and brimstone now, the stage is a mess;
    Of course, the only one worth all that
Trouble is always the bad one. So who do you think
    Is going to get the loudest applause
This time? A prima donna? Or two? The tenor? Again?

One, Two, Three (But Mostly a Lot of Etcs.)

1)
the more we talked
mostly he talked, this
sensible-looking man, with great, heralding
jaw structure and so
rather too quickly
we got around to the benign-looking woman
he had married, who
while in the pinkish-beige angora
sweater he hated so much, had proposed
to him.

2)
the other
evening a man came to fix the details
in my health insurance
plan and broke down on the sofa.

3)
Urs comes from
up near Andermatt and says
what people say to him up there
doesn't mean the same
to him
as what people say to him down here.

4)
78% of all men and 26% of all
women do this, do that
in this country or that, all
the time or some of the time;
24% of some of the men and 69%
of most women in some places
in most countries do this and that
and sometimes more that than
this, but rarely this and that
at any one given time, at any one
given place in most countries
according to some surveys.

5)
when someone's out there ranting at me
I pull out the old hat trick and
picture him naked
or on the can; when I go to the sauna
the men are there with their soggy
newspapers
over their tender little parts, so
what's the purpose of going to the sauna?

6)
the poetry shelves are not quite
bare around here, so I got ahold of something
new from the States —
it was vacuum-packed and didn't taste of anything;
that's when I began to get really
worried.

7)
in moments of need, I have cried
I admit
into a man's smooth, clean
pocket-warmed handkerchief —
washed, soaked in softener and ironed
by his mother.

8)
a hot dog with mustard and ketchup
no, instead of the
ketchup, chili sauce
plus loads of pickle
relish and dill pickle slices on a warmed bun
is what I fear my first
man loved
better than me.

9)
there's some pretty solid-looking
nightwear around here
planned I guess for women who
stand at stoves flipping things.

10)
Ach, Du liebe Schweiz!
generally speaking
I'd prefer to laugh
more.

11)
rows of black patent leather
pumps on sale —
bodyless swaying women.

12)
Marie Antoinette, at the crossroads
of her life, sat down
one morning on the grass
between breakfast and the fleecy sheep;
"Well", she said to her ladies
who were waiting
"That was that!" wherewith, up she got
and trotted slightly off
towards her Trianon.

13)
beneath a cross-stitched God Bless This Home
we got to discussing
ecological awareness
garbage sorting, compost heaps —
the sorted Swiss garbage collection system.

The Word Picnickers

makes me think of people who work
on clean-up committees
at, say, Ox Roasts or
on heat-charged, muggy park days.
Hospital volunteers in junior
high, or just brought up that way?

Roses in the Memorial Park
have fancy names, have
Japanese beetles and need
professional help -- the roses
droop and smell of downtown living rooms
in darkened summerness.

"Bales of straw" think the picnickers, sitting
on grass with fresh sandwiches,
fruit pie; cooler plunked down
heavy and bright blue. Big
grass stains in the wrong places
later on certain people, while

locusts, whatever else makes noises,
watch over the park roses and
some picnickers snooze, loll.

My Homecoming Drive-Around

Throughout the county there's rain in hills
With small after-dinner mint clapboard houses.
Auntie gets a red light type of old-fashioned nodding experience
So we avoid Route 30 East, at all costs.
Tobacco barns stand tall with their slats open.
Cornshock time's coming with Ham Suppers planned
And just this side of the bridge we learn
Able-bodied homecomers will surely be roped in.
Younger generations spark off some confusion:
Do those pastel places still serve black raspberry ice cream?
We pass the old school and Uncle Dwight, the janitor,
Gets stuck on the notion of maintenance supplies
While a new tale unfolds, in the back seat with the windows
Halfway, into the ultimate I told you so.

All along the roads there are white-washed tree trunks
Washington slept here taverns with plaques and
Confusion in the car over landmarks, local issues.
There's rain up in the hills and covered farm-produce stalls.
Younger generations of Miss Pennsylvanias
Play with Barbies beside shadows
In a town where the Greek Revival Courthouse
had one of its worst setbacks in the New World.
Long after we hit a postcard stand at an all you can eat place
Someone says, "Penn State produces the best weather weenies."
Nobody's listening because we've jolted into a big
Bang-up breakdown, smack in the middle of the heartland.
Throughout the county there's a fair amount of natural silence
No electricity and just plain no phones.

The Big Necklace Dream

Last night's dream brought me right up close to a peering face,
  quizzically
Angled on a curved neck. Oh help! It's Maria de Medici come back
  from the dead!
But, no, no, it was me dressed for a fancy ball, with things like
  chocolate
Wrappers laced in my hairdo, my bodice all studded
With glitzy doodads. Someone, bedoozled on a glass of something
Pink and fluffy, said, "Your necklace is missing!" and instantly my
  gown
Turned back into that trusty old, easy to iron, white uniform
With its pre-creased smile of compassion.
People began to watch. A puffy little man pushed his
Way through to me, asked if I had a special work sort of permit,
  how
Had I gotten in? Was I a nurse kind of woman? A few of the faces
  looked
As though they cared but my mouth couldn't find the language.
A woman took me aside, said we'd better get me fitted out
With a necklace, or hadn't I noticed
Everybody had one. The man kept harping about credentials and I
  couldn't decide
Whose final judgement was the one to count. The man had started
  me
Worrying about this permit thing: where was
Mine? Was it even the right color? How much did I have left? Valid
is a word like credentials. Meanwhile the woman said my necklace
Had to be searched for, chosen with care. What would I like
From this jagged, small land? She'd take me up a mountain, leave
  me to have
My own commemorative look around.

The lake lies at an angle it seems from up here. No noise, no push,
  fumes
No mess. I'm an ice princess in a simple, clean uniform, holding,
Of all things, a pluviometer. No music, no rain, no place
For pictures, just wind from all directions. A heavy
Black worm crawls alone along the curve
Of a blue-shadowed valley. That's it! To the woman, who's back

Again, I'm explaining I got mesmerised
By its lights. She puts *train traveling at night* on her list.
All the valleys fill up and there's a lot of noise. The party doors

Open inward, yellow and warm. A young, dark man, small
And bald, says, "It's Saturday night, for God's sake!" His gold
Earring wiggles, his arms are open. Someone gives me
The right mini-batteries for my model train's
String of lit windows.
They actually work, I'm lit up and blinking colors for Christmas!
There's a Gregorian chant going on in one corner and a jazz
    woman quavering
About what all she'd do in the name of love, if only, if
Only, so someone yells, "Hey, there! Nonny-nonny!" and even the
Milling, skinny, pot-bellied women with too much
Face powder stop sighing. What a theme park sense of timing!
The puffy, hot and bothered little man is drawn
To my necklace; his own is tarnished clumps
Of buttons that warn there is to be
Yet another, stiffer change of policy. But now
I'm past worrying over eager VERBOTEN signs , those dark
Warning, pickpocket sort of signs in, say, the National
Gallery, Notre-Dame, in Hauptbahnhof Zürich and the minds of
    many.
My party's warm with lit-up necklaces you've never
Dreamt the likes of before and people
Are getting along. My dark, smiling man says, "We're in this
    together." and
Given the setting, that seems profound, sounds hand in hand sen-
    sible.

When I wake up, I'm in a place different
people call home. They say I've finally come home and they're
    glad I'm home.

Train Poem

You think you're ready for the next gioco
when you find yourself realizing there will never
be another Fellini, never another
Masina, no more Fellini/Masina; just as you
know that for all those people rushing to the trains
there will be a coffin, at some time, of one material
or another; but you don't think about it for long.
Just as you don't think of their each and every
birth; so many births and each with a
name, some of which are, invariably,
identical.

Your train pulls out and passes
through time and Lenzburg, Aarau, Bern on time as the
minute hands of station clocks nationwide
move simultaneously and you don't see the end of it;
instead you pass an atomic power plant, spring green
forests, buildings with delivery trucks, then wives'
gardens and, once in a while, a bit of land nobody wants;
then along mountains with entrances and military
places you're not supposed to know about.

With earrings dangling you get off
at the station of your choice and you're right up
against all those people again, rushing to the dentist, with
shopping or children to meet yet more people, another train;
you move so close you bump into
individuals.

So What Is

So what is
this thing people are forever
running around
frantically after?
Griping and running to
beat the light,
right out in front of trams;
running to the hairdresser's,
to work or always to the doctor's.

It must be a notion: a belief
like a tree with green leaves
in a light-splattered crevice
of the personal deep dark;
or maybe some hope of making
late sunny afternoon love
in the woods on last year's
dry crispy leaves.
(What! In this day and age?)

And that's the whole problem:
this desire
creeping up to go hunting for
something like seashells
in a desert.
Is happiness, then, the absence
of impossible dreams?
Just one seashell
whole and divinely perfect,
to hold.

Mushrooms and the Man

What am I
    doing, someone like my mother
might ask, in Oensingen, Kanton Solothurn,
      in the middle of a man's kitchen, listening to opera!
          Do I know what I'm doing? Oh yes,
yes and so does he and
      that's something: two people in a room with food and music
who actually know what they want, how and when.

        He's cooking and I'm watching and we're drinking
spumante at the foot of the first
          chain of the Jura
    in his bold statement of a lover-cook's kitchen.
Bless him, the man loves all this operatic Italian stuff, too; we toast
to "Libiamo ne' lieti calici" on this,
          our dark October Grand Opera night:
      Verdi, Rossini, Bellini, Donizetti, Puccini
with mascarpone, improvizazioni and coloratura embellishments.
          I'm nowhere near those old
Velveeta/Spam toasted sandwiches. No!
      He even cooks by candlelight. Respiro! Oh!
His golden Shakespeare earring wiggles, hands intent
    in his mushroom-gathering basket --
a boleto here, a cantarello there -- prize funghi
    straight from the forest for me tonight.
      "Questa o quella", "Una furtiva lagrima",
    between the arias, instead of applause,
we hear the through train.
        Il Barbiere and we comment, the poor
    person on the prestissimo piccolo, that exposed

      French horn. This small dark warm
man's explaining how you don't wash
      mushrooms, you rub
them clean and take as much care with these
        miracles of nature
   as
is usually applied to tenors (Oh, the demanding roles!),
    while Germont, the younger

sings of joys in the country
and can't guess what's coming.

The funghi are doing their trick and this
is no longer so operatic, no longer Oensingen;
it's somewhere around Paradise before
that unfortunate apple episode.
It's the kind of thing you once in a great while
get very close to. Let him
sing "E lucevan le stelle" really late and loud and scare
the neighbors,
we've banished all misery from the plots; the music remains,
the wine-red velvet curtain.

Love Poem

I you and our sunny days' mood in this fuzzy what world
With a you and an I and a mostly mainly only
On a "Hey, Du, what's up?" kind of big morning;
The inside outside all around do-se-do of you
In our wild so let me list the ways world with
No more how now endings on the cold
Soft shoulders of streamy loveless byways,
Only maestoso poem picnics under the duvet,
Hilarious high-muck-a-muck promises and major
Nose-thumbing at the busy world of busy village bodies;
Signs of our futuristic you me us us us achievements
In Ferris wheel frames in our who home where the word
"Soul" flaps around a promisingly sentimental
Late night soft-footed jazz dance all of its own envisioning.

Fedora, You Can Tell

Fedora, you can tell, is thinking in the general
kitchen clutter sort of way, inwardly
tossing and turning, stamping and
frowning — Whoa, Starlight, whoa! — with worry.

Dorli starts shuffling her weight around into
portions of controlled winks and Marta

shakes her head over possible
swerves and derailings of uncareful love words.

Emma believes, as we all know, in basically putting
one foot in front of the other, as long as you still can.

Veronique doesn't notice and Gabi doesn't know.
Vreni keeps coming back to the favorite

spot on her mental figure-eight and that's men.
Sibyl's busy on her cellular, while Monika goes on and

on about invisible parts that can break off and go, oh
so wrong, so Petra thinks it's time
to take out her photographing equipment
and start snapping the lake.

I, in their midst,
                    was thinking of my man's
golden earring dangling
                    and tickling my nose —
up and down, up down, whoops! Ohhhhh!

Here I am holding on
                    to the spangled blade
          of a celestial whirligig
in a virtual reality star-dust installation:
                    throwing cares
to the wind, just this once, what the hell, and hanging
          on for dear life, whizzing;

skirt flaring out with real
        haute couture savoire faire,
           while the wind sings, "Well,
      if this isn't the ultimate look at
old Starlight now kind of flying high experience!"
        And I can feel it, I tell you, this
           is going down in Swiss history.
God, the luminous mystical sensations,
          constellations and the whole firmament!

In a moment I'll be reaching out
for one of those starry-eyed stratospheric things
to keep under a bell jar
to prove that this —
you'd better believe it yourself, at least
for a short while — really happened.

The Madonna of the Strawberries Finally Gets Her Two Cents' Worth in About Immobility, the Women's Movement and that Age-Old Status Quo Problem

The *Madonna in den Erdbeeren* (ca. 1425) hangs in the Kunstmuseum Solothurn, in Solothurn, Switzerland at the top of the stairs, on your right, unless they've moved it.

Once I ran barefoot on velvet green lawns, played tag with my sisters, dressed up in Mother's discarded ball gowns and combed my long golden hair in the late afternoon sunshine. I was brought up right and sang all the right songs for guests. Until one day a man, with an artistic smile, came along and captured me, told me to go get my best brocade (which I did), hold this big red book (which I did) and a fresh pale rose in my right hand (which I did). They got a hold of my sister's baby girl because she was so cute and had just about learned to stand and they told me to hold the rose out towards her. Her name is Grünlinde but they kept calling her Baby Jesu. Then the man gave me his old cloak and told me to sit on the wall (which I did) so as to save my legs (which it did) and not move (which I didn't). But I realized too late, just like Eve, that that was a dumb move; I'd been had and, of course, I got stuck with it ever since. A girl put in the garden for life, I've been sitting here for centuries now and this rose has only gotten heavier with time. First my limbs fell asleep, then went numb and cold and then all but fell off. There was a time I thought they had turned to marble but after a while I gave up, put mind over matter and have been holding up nicely ever since; this gives me a sense of belonging to those other women out there, the patient prostitutes, the daughters, to say nothing of the long-suffering wives and mothers, who otherwise couldn't get by. I used to worry a little about baby Grünlinde's circulation after I noticed that her outstretched hand was definitely greyer than the other. But she just keeps on smiling her sweet little smile so I guess she's okay. I don't know anything about babies. Except where they come from, in case you thought I was just some pretty little naive idiot, sitting here on this wall. I know a few things and I am observant. I know that a girl has to watch out for any kind of angel-wing flapping figure, who might fall out of the sky with a booming voice and give you some big news. Know all about that ex Maria virgine bit; they set it to music sometimes. Almost sounds like a joke but in actual fact, I am a virgin. The artistic guy, who crossed our sun-striped lawns that afternoon so long ago and turned my head, never even spoke to me much. It seems he had some sort of pathologically erotic experience with his paintbrush and all those globs of gooey pigment on his palette and that suited him just fine. But let's give credit where it's due — after all, he did a great job on my baby niece and me, capturing the depth in our dark eyes and the fine strands of our fiery hair. And we've ended up doing a lot for the reputation of the museum (town, even) that we've finally come to hang in. How many artists you know, have done to a piece of wood 145.5 cm x 87 cm what he did with, say, the violet leaves? The gold-leaf clouds with their dragontail-like swirls? Or the strawberry blossoms, the berries ripe enough to pick? What's-his-name was inspired, day after day, by what he saw during his stay under our roof and I, for one, was glad it was taking him so many months; he painted in the rose bushes, violets, lilies of the valley, snowdrops, strawberries, etc. and birds, copying Mother's "meditation garden" (that's what she called it — behind her back, we called it her "lovers' garden"). But he has all the plants blooming at once, which goes to show how much you can trust an artist. Maybe he was merely reflecting some warped vision of the Lord's garden, some unnatural Paradise. I've been called an uppity virgin, for my attitude. But I've been called much worse. All hell broke loose when praise of this portrait of me and little Grünlinde got about; it reached a little too far and especially far too wide for our family's male comfort. You see, my sister's baby wasn't her husband's and she suddenly got scared and pushed Grünlinde off as mine real quick, even though all the women in the house knew exactly what had been going on. When questions began to arise in marketplaces, the men in the family turned on me, publicly, and their blame came down on me real hard. This artist guy, who'd turned my whole life around that first sunny afternoon, was gone overnight and, naturally, he didn't leave his name. And baby Grünlinde and I? Well, paint speaks for itself, doesn't it? It's been no big consolation, however, that the portrait was such a hit, was blessed and the whole bit, nor that my own story has been such a deep source of inspiration for, plays, poems, you name it. Real life! Well, *my* real space is a shade cramped, especially for the two of us, for much longer anyway, and you can't eat the strawberries. But a girl shouldn't complain — my destiny's a lot better than all those other virgins who have to stand *and* hold the baby *and* look stupid. Furthermore, we both look pretty spiffy for our age. I'd give anything, though, just to get up and pace along the wall for a few minutes, at night, say. And this dimension sure has stunted baby Grünlinde's growth something ferocious!

Moon Over Oensingen

When the moon was somewhere between
three-quarters and full,
a soft-sounding voice slithered out
and left its sisters
hanging up there in a sphere.

The voice was so small (insignificant, some narrators
might write, nothing
more than an idea) that the moon
hardly noticed and so went on shining just as before, and
no one looking up
would have seen anything astray.

The voice that got away landed on the red-polished big toenail
of a woman, at last peacefully sleeping near her lover,
and in this manner it quietly entered the bone, from where
it traveled to the rib cage and on to other
complex bone setups.
The voice carried a dance in its lungs —
no tango, no waltz, no quick sashays,
but large slow loops in the colors of the Olympics.
Feeling something slight here and there, the woman
began to dream, for no reason at all, of the painting called
Wenn die Vernunft schläft, singen die Sirene
by Max Ernst, seeing as he must have, a yellow
ruffly rosette-thing hovering in a green background high
above a lavender dot-thought, which had sunk deep into the blue.

During all this, the voice looped around a few more nooks and
    crannies
and paused and pondered.
The woman heard the voice distinctly when it moved the slightest:
she began to think in her dream,
started worrying the voice might infiltrate her bloodstream
and she would be left
not knowing what to do.
She moved her toes, her thighs, then her head and was not afraid.

The woman got up from bed and looked out the kitchen window

of her lover's condominium
in Oensingen
at the Perpetual Moon Mother dispersing pale
elongated clouds from the black sky to the music
of obscure saxophones in such a manner that the woman
was induced to sit down and make her own calculations,
right then and there, in the light of the moon.

On Reading Walt Whitman But Not Too Much

> The earth does not argue,
> Is not pathetic, has no arguments,
> Does not scream, haste, persuade, threaten, promise
>
> Walt Whitman
> from "Song of the Rolling Earth"

I think of the earth out there all winter
        on her own, no wonder
        it takes her so long
            coming into spring. Everything
is green and people on the sidewalks look finally
happy; they must feel grateful, knowing
        the earth is a big patient lady,
        like a sturdy-necked image
            of Helvetia, flickering
on a child's paper lantern for the first of August.
When spring at last gets a good grip
        on itself, there's no
        holding back and you can
            almost hear the sun
rip open fuzzy buds all over the Mittelland.

Despite this particular spring, these openings
        without recourse, I see places I need to be.

Rapsfelder turn their awful angular
        yellow and stun me
        as never before, pinned
            as they are, helplessly
against a sky, blue or black threatening.
I already picture men playing dominoes in the shade
        of tall oleander on a plaza
        somewhere with a different
            push within the seasons.